Materials & Supplies

Thread: We recommend nylon monofilament thread, better known as Nymo. Size B works best, as many passes can be made through the seed beads with it, while still accommodating both the thread and needle. Nymo does not need any conditioning, as it is not prone to fraying or twisting. We've also used Superlon thread, also known as S-lon, with great results.

Both threads come on spools and cones in a wide variety of colors. Neutral colors, such as black, white, tan, and gray can be used for the warp threads. We recommend using weft threads in colors that coordinate with whatever bead color falls to the outside edges of the woven piece, as this will help hide the thread. If desired, a permanent maker can always be used to color the outer threads to match the beads. Be cautious when using transparent beads, as the thread color may distort or enhance the original bead color.

Needles: Generally, a long thin needle with a narrow eye works best for loom work. We use Clover Needlecraft Incorporated's Beading Needles numbers 10–13. In addition, a simple needle threader is handy for ushering the thread through the needle eye, and a short needle is useful for hiding warp threads.

Seed beads: Seed beads are a class of beads that are the smallest glass beads—not all seed beads are created equal! Common sizes include 15/0, 11/0, 8/0, and 6/0. We've found that Japanese seed beads are the most uniform, making them the best for weaving. In addition, the depth of color range and finishes for these beads is most extensive. Uniform beads result in elegant and even loom work with a silky, smooth texture. Using different types of seed beads in one weaving will throw off the uniformity of the finished piece.

The projects in this book use size 11/0 Toho seed beads exclusively. The type of bead used (Round or Treasure [a slightly squared cylinder]) and the bead color is shown on the bead placement charts for each project.

Scissors: Choose a small pair of scissors with a nice sharp tip.

Here, light silver round beads have been used in a design that also contains cylindrical beads. As a result of using two different types of beads, the rows are becoming uneven.

The bracelet on the right uses 11/0 Toho Treasure (cylinder) beads, while the bracelet on the left uses 11/0 Toho Round beads.

The outer edges of the right bracelet are uneven, due to mixing round and cylindrical beads. The left bracelet uses beads of the same type, resulting in a uniform, professional look.

3

The Loom Basics
Part Names and Functions

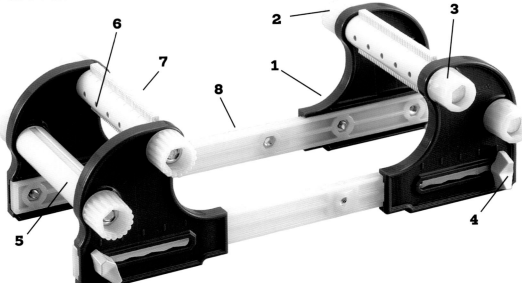

1. Frame
2. Release knobs A (loosen or tighten the beams)
3. Release knobs B (rotate the beams)
4. Adjustment screws (allow adjustment of rail length between warp guide beams)
5. Winding beams (keep ends of warp threads in place and wind long pieces)
6. Peg holes (for use with the Continuous Warp Method, see page 6)
7. Warp guide beams (beams with grooves to guide the warp threads)
8. Rails

Grooves

The warp guide beams contain two different types of grooves:

Grooves (a): Use for cylinder beads (size 11/0). The maximum width of your woven piece will be about 2⁹⁄₁₆" (6.5cm) wide, or 43 beads across (44 warp threads).

Grooves (b): Use for round beads (size 11/0). The maximum width of your woven piece will be about 2½" (6.5cm) wide, or 39 beads across (40 warp threads). Grooves (b) can be identified by the horizontal line running along the base of the grooves.

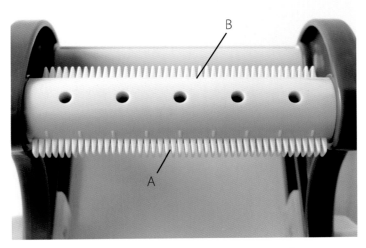

The warp guide beam contains two different types of grooves for working with different types of beads: grooves a (bottom), and grooves b (top).

Additional parts

Pegs (12): Use for Continuous Warp Method (see page 6)

Warp thread stoppers (2): Insert stopper into holes in the grooves on the warp guide beam. Keeps the warp threads from popping off the grooves while loom is in use or moved.

Non-slip strips (4): Stick on bottom of loom to prevent slippage while weaving.

Holders (4): Use these to keep warp threads in place on winding beam. Also, use serrated edge to untangle warp threads.

Beading needle No. 10 and threader (1)

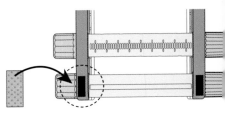

How to Adjust the Loom

Use the indicators on the rails and elongated slits to adjust the length of the loom in ⅜" (1cm) units.

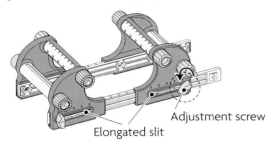

Loosen right and left adjustment screws.

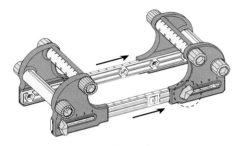

Move frames to desired length.

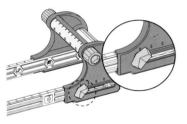

Set frames at the desired length; then tighten adjustment screws on both sides. Make sure the frame is set at the same position on both rails before tightening the screws.

Shortest position: 2¼" (5.5cm)

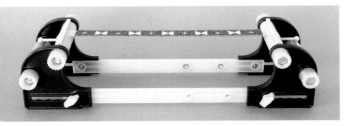

Longest position: 8⅜" (21.5cm)

How to Use Release Knobs A & B

1 Loosen beam with Knob A (counter clockwise).

2 Rotate beam with Knob B

3 Tighten beam with Knob A, making sure the beam is firmly set.

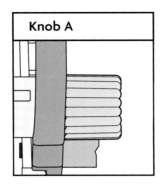

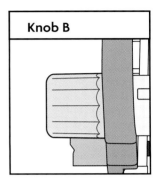

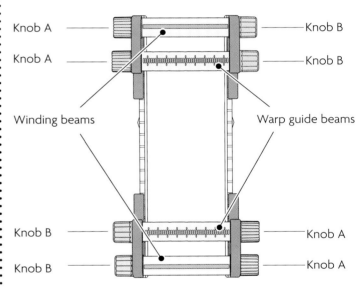

Important!

Check the knobs to make sure they are firmly tightened while weaving. Loose knobs may result in uneven weaving.

The Continuous Warp Method

Warp the Loom

Use this warping method for shorter woven pieces, 7½" (19cm) long or less.

1 Adjust the length of the loom to fit the piece you plan to weave. Insert a peg in one of the peg holes in each warp guide beam.

2 Secure one end of the warp thread on the winding beam with a holder, and loop the thread around the peg 2–3 times to start the warping process.

3 Place the warp thread into a groove on the warp guide beam and extend the thread to the corresponding groove on the opposite beam, looping it around from left to right. Repeat until you have the necessary number of warp strands. Note: The number of warps strands required will be 1 more than the number of beads you plan to use across the body of your work, so a project 11 beads wide requires 12 warp strands.

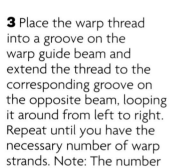

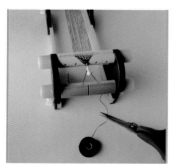

4 After placing the required number of warp strands, loop the end of the warp thread around the closest peg 2–3 times. Secure the thread on the closest winding beam with a holder and trim the end.

5 Insert the warp thread stoppers into the holes in the grooves of each warp guide beam. This will keep the warp threads from popping out of the grooves.

How to Start Weaving

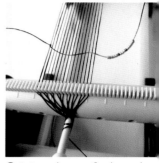

1 Thread the weft thread onto a beading needle, leaving a 4" (10cm) tail. Tie the loose end onto the leftmost warp thread.

2 Bring the weft thread UNDER the warp threads and pick up the beads for the first row.

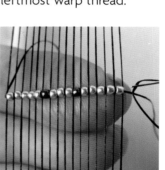

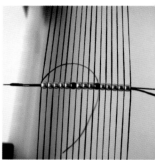

3 Press the beads up against the warp threads, positioning one bead between each warp thread, starting from the left.

4 While continuing to hold the beads in place against the warp threads, slide the needle back through beads, needle eye first, making sure the needle passes OVER all of the warp threads.

Important!

When you pass the eye of the needle through the beads, always bring it OVER the warp threads.

5 Repeat Steps 2–4 to continue adding rows of beads until your design is complete. After you have finished the last row, tie the weft thread to the warp thread.

Hiding Warp & Weft Threads

Method A

Use this finishing method for a project that uses one continuous thread as the warp and has no increases or decreases.

1 To remove the woven piece, release the warp beams. Remove the holders; then remove the pegs.

2 Place the woven piece on a flat surface. Divide the warp threads at the center.

3 Pull strand 1 downward gently, as shown in Figure 1.

4 Pull strand 2 upward (see Figure 1). Repeat Steps 3 and 4 until you reach the left edge of the piece.

5 Repeat the same process on the right side, working out from the center as you did before (see Figure 2).

6 To hide the warp threads that have been pulled through the piece, thread the end of the left thread onto a beading needle. Pass the needle through the second bead from the left side, going through 2 or 3 beads. Pass needle through 4 to 5 rows of the weft threads, picking up the UPPER weft threads. Pass the needle through a row of beads from left to right, going through the second bead from the right side. Then, pass the needle through the next row of beads, going back to the left. Cut thread at the edge of the second to last bead in the row (see Figure 3). Repeat with the remaining warp thread.

7 Hide the weft threads at the beginning and end of the woven piece as shown in Figure 4.

Weaver's Knot

When you run out of weft thread, join more thread by using the Weaver's Knot. Make sure the knot slips inside the beads.

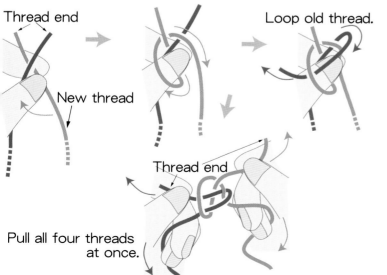

Thread end

New thread

Loop old thread.

Thread end

Pull all four threads at once.

Figure 1

Weft thread at the end of the piece

Warp thread

④ ②
⑤ ③
① Center

Figure 2

Warp thread

⑥ ⑧
⑦ ⑨

Figure 3

Upper weft thread

Lower weft thread

Bead

Warp thread

Figure 4

Important!

We cannot express strongly enough here that if the warp threads do not pull easily STOP. Try following Method B on page 8, which requires the warp threads only be pulled downward through the piece. If it is not possible to pull the warp threads through the piece at all, trim the warp thread loops, keeping the threads long enough to be threaded onto a needle. Then, follow the method described on page 10 to hide the individual warp threads in the woven piece.

Method B

Use this finishing method for a project with a continuous warp thread and increases or decreases on only one end of the woven piece. The warp threads will all be pulled downward toward the increase/decrease end, cut, and then woven back into the piece.

1 Remove the woven piece from the loom and place it on a flat surface. Pull threads 1–3 downward toward the end with the increase or decrease, following the arrows in Figure 1. Do NOT pull on the outer warp threads (labeled A and B). Continue pulling strands 1–3 downward gently until the thread loops meet the beads in the top row without causing it to pucker. Cut the thread loops at the bottom (see Figure 2).

2 Thread one of the outer warp threads on a beading needle. If the piece has increases or decreases, pick up UPPER weft threads for several rows, starting at the first full row. Then, run the needle through the closest row of beads, bringing it out at the side. Cut the thread at the edge of the second to last bead in the row. Hide the remaining outer warp thread in the same way (see Figure 3).

3 With the exception of the threads marked with stars, hide the remaining wrap threads using the method described in Step 2 (see Figure 4).

4 The starred threads are on the last row. To hide these threads, thread them on a beading needle. Then, pick up the UPPER weft threads for several rows, starting with the second to last row (see Figure 5). Run the needle through a row of beads as shown in Figure 3, and trim the excess thread.

5 Hide the weft threads at the beginning and end of woven piece as shown in Figure 4 of Method A on page 7.

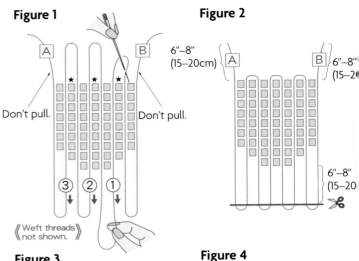

Figure 1

Don't pull.   Don't pull.

《Weft threads not shown.》

Figure 2

6"–8" (15–20cm)

6"–8" (15–2

6"–8" (15–20

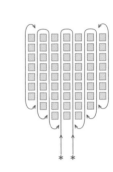

Figure 3

Figure 4

Tip

When moving the needle horizontally, avoid passing it through the same beads twice.

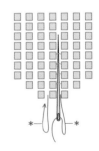

Figure 5

Glossary of Terms

If you're new to beading or bead weaving, you might not be as familiar with some of the terms used in this book. Here is a short list of the most important terms you'll need to know:

Bead tips: These are used to finish the end of a piece by enclosing the working strands. They also provide a way to attach a clasp to a project. See how to attach a bead tip on page 12.

Clasp: This is any closure used to attach the ends of a finished project. Clasps come with two halves, one to be attached to each end of a completed jewelry piece.

Increases/Decreases: A project is said to have increases or decreases when the number of beads per row is raised or lowered, usually at the beginning and end of the project.

Jump rings: These are small metal rings with a split, allowing them to be opened and closed. They are most often used to connect two different items, like a bead tip and a clasp. See how to work with jump rings on page 12.

The Multiple Warp Method

Warp the Loom

Use this warping method for longer woven pieces, 7½" (19cm) long or longer.

1 Cut the number of warp threads desired to the length of the woven piece plus 16" (40.5cm). Group the threads on one winding beam and secure them in place with a holder. Pull gently on the threads to ensure they are held in place. Trim the ends to about ¼" (0.5cm).

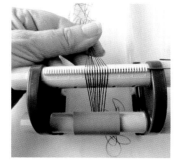

2 Position each warp thread into a grove on the warp guide beam. Then, slide the warp thread stopper over the threads through the holes in the grooves.

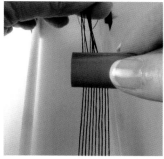

3 Turn the loom so you can work on the other end. Comb the loose ends of the warp threads with the serrated edge of the holder to separate them. Repeat Step 2 with the loose ends of the warp threads and the other end of the loom. Do not secure the threads with a holder yet.

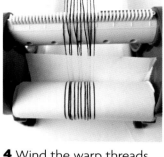

4 Wind the warp threads onto the winding beam with the holder. First, loosen Knob A on the winding beam; then rotate Knob B. To ensure the warp threads wind evenly, place a slip of paper the width of the warp plus ⅜" (1cm) on each side between the warp threads and the winding beam. Wind the threads until a tail approximately 4" (10cm) long is left on the warp threads on the opposite end.

5 Pull the warp threads tight and secure the loose ends onto the second winding beam with a holder. Pull gently on the threads to ensure they are held in place. Trim the ends of the warp threads to about ¼" (0.5cm).

6 Wind the warp threads around the second winding beam, adjusting the tension of the warp threads. Then, tighten Knob A on both winding beams to hold the warp threads at the desired tension.

Round beads: These are seed beads with a rounded shape.

Treasure beads: These are seed beads with a slightly cylindrical shape.

Warp: The series of threads that run lengthwise through a woven piece and are held in place by a frame or loom.

Weft: The working thread woven widthwise through the warp of a woven piece; in bead weaving, the thread used to attach beads to the warp.

How to Start Weaving

Using the Multiple Warp Method, you must start weaving at the end of the loom that has the least amount of warp thread wrapped around the winding beam (the end without the paper). Once you've identified the proper end at which to begin weaving, you can follow the process described in How to Start Weaving for the Continuous Warp Method (see page 6).

Hiding Warp & Weft Threads

Weft

To hide the weft threads at the beginning of the woven piece:

1 Pass the needle through 1–3 beads.

2 Pick up the UPPER weft threads for 4–5 rows, beginning at the second row from the end.

3 Pass the needle through the nearest row of beads, and cut the thread at the edge of the last bead.

To hide the weft threads at the end of the woven piece:

1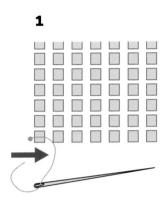

2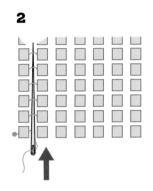

3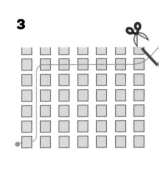

1 After you have woven the last row, tie the weft thread to the outer warp thread once and hide the end following Steps 1–3 above.

1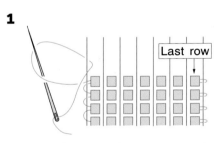

Warp

1 Hide the warp threads using the method described in Step 6 of Method A in Hiding Warp & Weft Threads for the Continuous Warp Method (see page 7). If the piece has no increases or decreases, when you pick up the weft threads, start with the second row from the end. Avoid picking up the weft threads in the end row.

1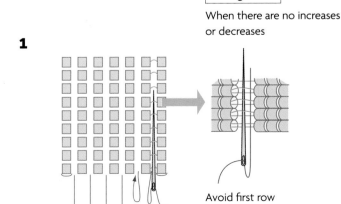

Enlargement

When there are no increases or decreases

Avoid first row

Increasing & Decreasing

This technique allows you to increase or decrease the number of beads in each row, while keeping the weft threads hidden.

Increasing

1 Bring the threaded needle UNDER the warp threads. Pick up the number of beads needed for the increase. For example, if you plan to increase the row by 1 bead at each end, pick up 1 bead. Press the increase bead(s) against the underside of the warp threads, positioning it between the threads, and bring the needle out as shown.

2 Pass the needle through the increase bead(s), eye first. Make sure to pass the needle OVER the warp threads.

3 Insert the needle under the warp threads, pick up the remaining beads needed to complete the row, and position them between the warp threads.

4 Working in the opposite direction, pass the needle, eye first, through all the beads in the row, including the increase bead(s). Repeat these steps as necessary for your project, following the Bead Placement Chart.

1
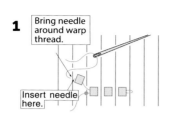
Bring needle around warp thread.
Insert needle here.

2
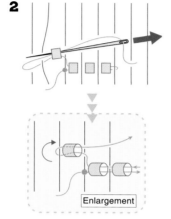
Enlargement

3
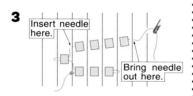
Insert needle here.
Bring needle out here.

4
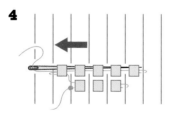

Decreasing

1 After completing the row before the decrease, catch the warp thread at the left edge with the needle.

2 Pass the needle through the last bead in the row before the decrease, eye first.

3 Bring the needle underneath the warp threads, and pass it through the beads of the decrease row. Press the beads up between the warp threads.

4 Pass the needle back through the beads of the decrease row, eye first. Repeat these steps as necessary for your project, following the Bead Placement Chart.

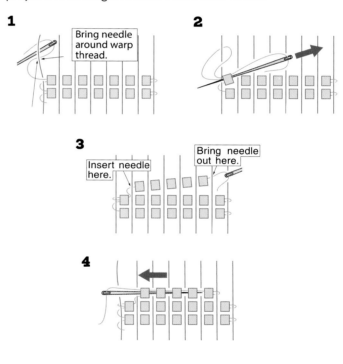

1 Bring needle around warp thread.

2

3 Insert needle here. Bring needle out here.

4

Hiding Warp & Weft Threads

Projects that have a continuous thread for the warp and increases or decreases at both ends can be finished almost the same way as described for Method B on page 8. For these projects, the warp threads cannot be pulled down through the piece as described in Step 1 of Method B. Instead, the loops formed by the warp threads must be trimmed at both ends of the project. Then, the individual warp threads can be hidden in the design following Steps 2–4 of Method B. Hide the weft threads following Figure 4 of Method A.

Additional Techniques

Dividing a Woven Piece

1 When you reach the point at which the work is to be divided, continue weaving the left side of the piece until you reach the end of the working warp section.

2 Add a new weft thread to weave the right side of the piece, hiding the end of the thread in the weaving as shown.

3 Use the new weft thread to weave the right side of the piece. When the right side is the same length as the left side, wind the woven piece around the winding beam to expose another working section of warp threads, and continue weaving both sides separately.

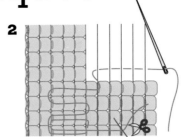
2

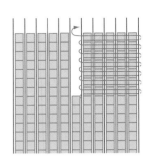
3

Joining the Ends of a Necklace

1 To begin, hide the inner warp threads as shown by passing the warp threads from one end of the necklace through several rows of the weft threads on the other end of the necklace. Then, pass the warp threads through the closest row of beads and trim. Avoid passing the needle through the same beads twice. Do this with the inner warp threads of each end of the necklace (see Figures 1–3).

2 Hide the outer warp threads by weaving them through several rows of beads on the opposite end of the necklace as shown. Trim the excess (see Figures 4–5).

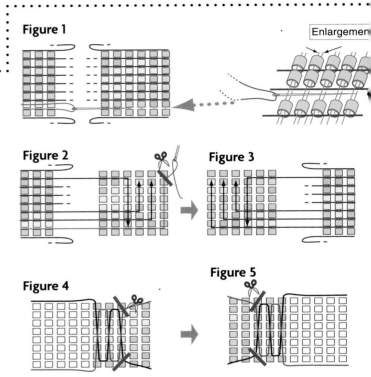
Figure 1   Enlargement
Figure 2   Figure 3
Figure 4   Figure 5

Attaching Jewelry Findings

Attaching a bead tip

1 Pass the thread through the bead tip and then through a bead. Knot the thread 2–3 times and apply a drop of glue. Trim the end.

2 Close the bead tip around the bead and thread end.

3 Form a ring using round-nose pliers. Make sure the ring is completely closed.

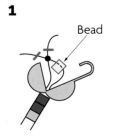
1   Bead

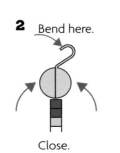
2   Bend here.   Close.

3

Working with jump rings

Make sure the ring is tightly closed with no space showing between the ends.

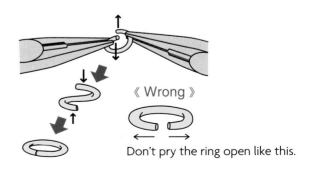
《 Wrong 》
Don't pry the ring open like this.

12

Attaching Fringe to a Straight Edge

1 Insert the needle in the third bead from the left in the end row, and bring it out at the second to last bead in the row. Leave a 6" (15cm) tail, and secure it with tape.

2 Following the project fringe chart, pick up the beads for the fringe.

3 Starting with the second bead from the bottom, pass the needle back through the fringe beads. You can also try the picot option by passing the needle back through the fringe beads starting with the fourth bead from the bottom.

4 Make the remaining fringe strands by repeating Steps 2 & 3 until you reach the edge of the woven piece.

5 After you've attached the last fringe strand, remove the tape from the beginning thread tail and tie the thread ends together tightly 2–3 times.

6 Run the thread ends through a few rows of beads and trim as shown.

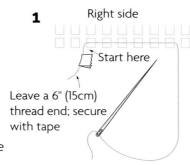

1 Right side
Start here
Leave a 6" (15cm) thread end; secure with tape

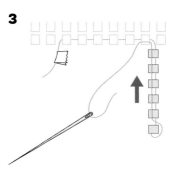

3

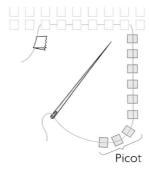

Picot option

Picot

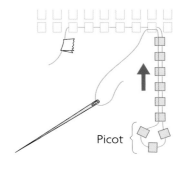

Picot

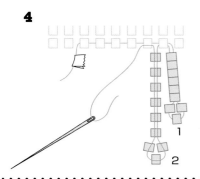

4

1
2

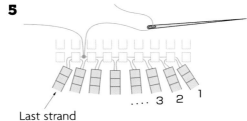

5

Last strand

.... 3 2 1

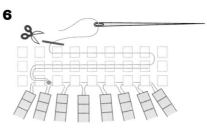

6

Sewing Side Seams

1 Fold the woven piece where indicated on the Bead Placement Chart. Pass a needle threaded with approximately 12" (30.5cm) of thread through the row of beads at the fold. Leave about half the length of the thread as a tail, securing it with a piece of tape.

2 Stitch one edge of the folded section together, weaving the needle through the beads as shown.

3 Hide the working end of the thread as shown. Remove the tape from the thread tail and repeat Steps 2 & 3 for the other side seam, using the thread tail.

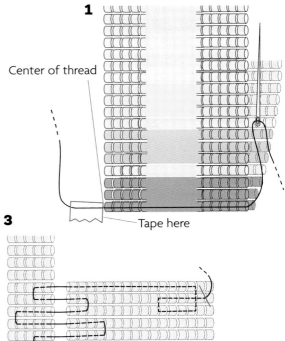

1 Back
Center of thread
Tape here

2

3

Ohio Star Pendant Necklace

By Carol C. Porter

1 Warp the loom with 1 continuous thread to form 16 warp strands using the Continuous Warp Method (see page 6).

2 Weave the design following the Bead Placement Chart (see below).

3 Hide the warp and weft threads using Method A (see page 7).

4 To finish, measure the desired length of one side of the necklace strand and add 5" (12.5cm). Cut two threads to this length. Thread the needle with both strands and string on the assorted beads to form one half of the necklace strand, leaving approximately a 3" (7.5cm) tail. Attach the strand to the necklace by threading the tail ends into the beads at the top of the pendant as shown. Tie the ends together and hide the thread. Repeat to form the other side of the necklace strand. Attach bead tips and jump rings to the ends of the strands using the methods described on page 12. Then, add the clasp.

Techniques:
Continuous Warp,
Straight Edge Finish
Beads: 15 across
Warp: 16

Supplies
- Beads (see Color Key and Bead Placement Chart)
- Assorted beads for necklace strand
- Nymo, size B in purple
- Beading needle & threader
- Scissors
- 2 bead tips
- 2 jump rings
- 1 closure set

Color Key: Using 11/0 Toho Round Beads

☐	557 Gold
■	252 Purple
▨	477 Lavender

Bead Placement Chart

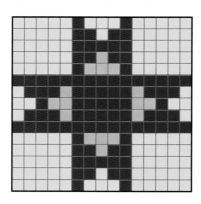

Attaching Necklace to Pendant

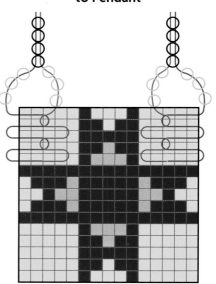

14

'Bead-Tangle" Pendant Necklace

By Fran Ortmeyer

1 Warp loom with 1 continuous thread to form 33 warp strands using the Continuous Warp Method (see page 6).

2 Weave the design following the Bead Placement Chart (see below).

3 Hide the warp and weft threads using Method A (see page 7).

4 Attach the pendant to the necklace strand by sewing the flap. To do this, turn the woven piece to the wrong side. Using a single thread, pass the needle through the beads in the first row and the last row of the flap section twice to secure a fold in the flap. Tie the thread ends together securely and hide them in the woven piece.

Bead Placement Chart

} Flap

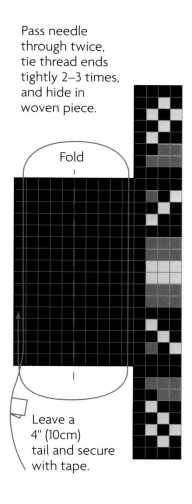

Pass needle through twice, tie thread ends tightly 2–3 times, and hide in woven piece.

Fold

Leave a 4" (10cm) tail and secure with tape.

Techniques: Continuous Warp, Straight Edge Finish
Beads: 32 across
Warp: 33

Supplies
- Beads (see Color Key and Bead Placement Chart)
- Nymo, size B in black
- Beading needle & threader
- Pre-purchased black suede cord necklace
- Scissors

Color Key: Using 11/0 Toho Treasure Beads

- ■ 49 Black
- ■ 25C Red
- ▢ 21C Silver

Silver & Blue Stripe Bracelet

By Fran Ortmeyer

Techniques: Continuous Warp, Straight Edge Finish, 1 Bead & Multi-Loop Closure
Beads: 10 across
Warp: 11

Supplies

- Beads (see Color Key and Bead Placement Chart)
- Nymo, size B in white
- Beading needle & threader
- Scissors
- Flat silver bead for closure

Color Key: Using 11/0 Toho Treasure Beads

- ▢ 21 Silver
- ■ 27BD Dark Metallic Blue

1 Warp the loom with 1 continuous thread to form 11 warp strands using the Continuous Warp Method (see page 6).

2 Weave the design following the Bead Placement Chart (at right).

3 Hide the warp and weft threads using Method A (see page 7).

4 Attach the bead and multi-loop closure as shown to the ends of the bracelet.

Bead Placement Chart

Last row →

Repeat 6 times

Row 1 →

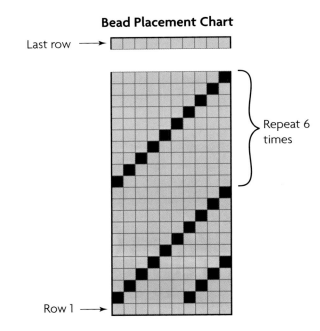

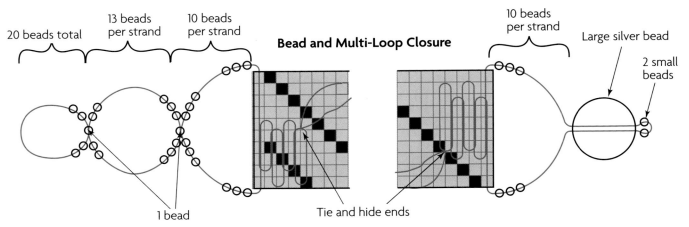

20 beads total

13 beads per strand

10 beads per strand

Bead and Multi-Loop Closure

10 beads per strand

Large silver bead

2 small beads

1 bead

Tie and hide ends

Oriental Fret Ornament Bracelet

By Carol C. Porter

1 Warp the loom with 1 continuous thread to form 16 warp strands using the Continuous Warp Method (see page 6)

2 Weave the design following the Bead Placement Chart (see below).

3 Hide the warp and weft threads using Method A (see page 7).

4 Attach the bead and loop closures. For the loops, weave in the end of a piece of thread, string on 15 beads, and then weave in the other end as shown. For the beads, weave in the end of a piece of thread, and string on 2 small beads, 1 large bead, and 2 small beads. Feed the thread back through the large bead and first 2 small beads. Then, weave in the end.

Attach Bead & Loop Closure

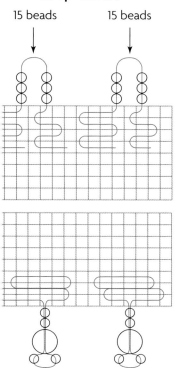

15 beads   15 beads

Techniques:
Continuous Warp,
Straight Edge Finish,
2 Bead & Loop Closures
Beads: 15 across
Warp: 16

Supplies

- Beads (see Color Key and Bead Placement Chart)
- Nymo, size B in black (Design 1)
- Nymo, size B in red (Design 2)
- Beading needle & threader
- Scissors
- 2 black beads for closure (Design 1)
- 2 yellow beads for closure (Design 2)

Color Key: Using 11/0 Toho Round Beads

- ☐ 122 Cream
- ◼ 1206 Turquoise
- ◼ 49 Black
- ☐ 1283 Tan

Color Key: Using 11/0 Toho Treasure Beads

- ◼ 48 Opaque Navy Blue
- ◼ 45A Opaque Cherry
- ☐ 42C Opaque Dandelion
- ◼ 47 Opaque Mint Green

Bead Placement Chart Design 1

Ending rows

Row 1 ⟶

Repeat 5 times

Bead Placement Chart Design 2

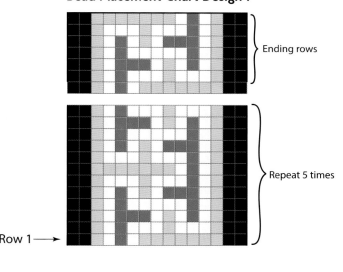

Last row ⟶

Repeat 7 times

Row 1 ⟶

17

Turquoise & Brown Bracelet & Earring Set

By Carol C. Porter

For bracelet:

1 Warp the loom with 1 continuous thread to form 14 warp strands using the Continuous Warp Method (see page 6)

2 Weave the design following the Bead Placement Chart (see below).

3 Hide the weft threads. Divide the warp threads into 3 groups. Feed the groups into the bead tips. Tie the ends of each group into a knot inside the bead tips. Attach the 3-hole headers as shown.

4 Attach the closure to the 3-hole headers.

For earrings:

1 Warp the loom with 2 sets of 10 warp strands using the Continuous Warp Method (see page 6).

2 Weave the design on each set of warp strands following the Bead Placement Chart (see below) to create 2 earrings.

3 Hide the warp threads on the bottom of the earrings only. Hide all the weft threads.

4 Divide the top warp threads into 2 groups and feed them through the bead tips. Tie off the ends of the threads, and attach 2-hole headers, following the same method as with the bracelet.

5 Attach the earring wires to the 2-hole headers.

Bracelet Bead Placement Chart

Row 43: Reverse and work rows 41–1

Row 41 →
Row 35 →

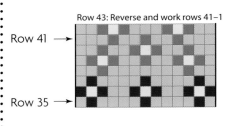

Row 20: Repeat rows 5–19

Row 19 →
Row 5 →
Row 1 →

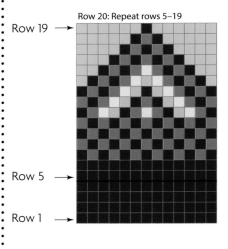

Earrings: Make 2 Bead Placement Chart

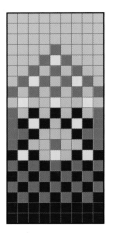

Random Sampler Cuff Bracelet

By Alyssa Vargas

Bead Placement Chart

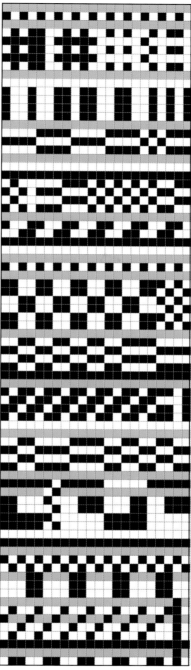

Techniques:

Continuous Warp,
Straight Edge Finish,
Attached Leather Cuff

Beads: 22 across
Warp: 23

Supplies

- Beads (see Color Key and Bead Placement Chart)
- Nymo, size B in black
- Beading needle & threader
- Lightweight black leather remnant, 9" x 3" (23 x 7.5cm)
- Leather needle
- Black sewing thread
- Black leather cord
- 6 eyelets
- Eyelet setting tools

Color Key: Using 11/0 Toho Round Beads

 49 Opaque Black

 44 Opaque Light Green

 41 Opaque White

1 Warp loom with 1 continuous thread to form 23 warp strands using the Continuous Warp Method (see page 6).

2 Weave the design following the Bead Placement Chart (at right).

3 Hide the warp and weft threads using Method A (see page 7).

4 Trim the leather cuff to size, and, using black sewing thread, sew the woven piece onto the leather.

5 Place three eyelets on each end of cuff. Thread the leather cord through the eyelets to form a lace-up closure.

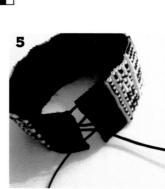

Bookmark

By Fran Ortmeyer

Techniques:
Continuous Warp,
Increasing and
Decreasing
Beads: 9 across
Warp: 10

Supplies
- Beads (see Color Key and Bead Placement Chart)
- Nymo, size B in black
- Beading needle & threader
- Scissors

Color Key: Using 11/0 Toho Treasure Beads

☐ IF Matte White

▨ 786 Light Purple

■ 116 Dark Purple

1 Warp the loom with 2 sets of 10 warp strands using the Continuous Warp Method (see page 6).

2 Weave the design on each set of warp strands following the Bead Placement Chart (see below) to create 2 bookmark ends.

3 Hide the warp and weft threads using the method described on page 11.

4 Measure the length of your book and add 6"–8" (15–20.5cm). Cut 2 threads to this length. Bead and attach the threads as a connecting chain to the two ends of the bookmark, using two threaded needles.

5 Weave the thread ends of the bookmark chain into the woven bookmark ends as shown.

Bead Placement Chart

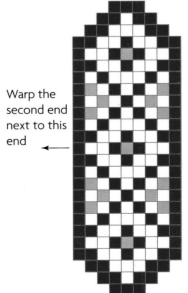

Warp the second end next to this end ←

Ataching the Chain to the Bookmark Ends

1 bead   5 beads per strand

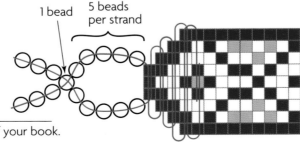

Continue making chain the length of your book. Weave in ends as at the beginning.

Use 2 needles

Ocean Waves Bracelet

By Carol C. Porter

Techniques:
Continuous Warp,
 Increasing and
Decreasing
Beads: 16 across
Warp: 17

Supplies

- Beads (see Color Key and Bead Placement Chart)
- Nymo, size B in turquoise
- Beading needle & threader
- Scissors
- 2 bead tips
- 2 jump rings
- 1 toggle closure

Color Key: Using 11/0 Toho Treasure Beads

☐	121 White
☐	21 Silver
☐	132 Aqua
☐	27BD Turquoise

1 Warp the loom with 1 continuous thread to form 17 warp strands using the Continuous Warp Method (see page 6).

2 Weave the design following the Bead Placement Chart (see below).

3 Hide the warp and weft threads using the method described on page 11.

4 Attach the findings using the method described on page 12.

Bead Placement Chart

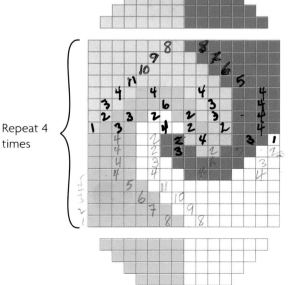

Repeat 4 times

Black-White Color Block Bracelet

By Carol C. Porter

Bead Placement Chart

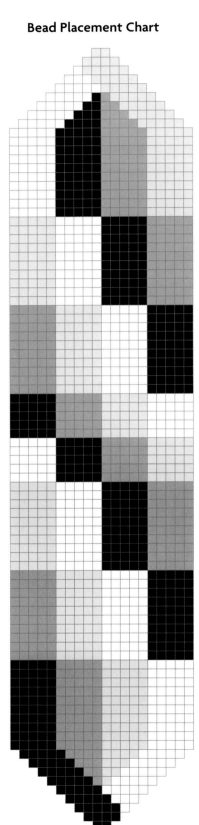

Techniques:
Continuous Warp,
Increasing and
Decreasing
Beads: 20 across
Warp: 21

Supplies

- Beads (see Color Key and Bead Placement Chart)
- Nymo, size B in white
- Beading needle & threader
- Scissors
- 2 bead tips
- 2 jump rings
- 1 closure set

Color Key: Using 11/0 Toho Treasure Beads

- 49 Black
- 29 Silver
- 21 Clear
- 121 White

1 Warp the loom with 1 continuous thread to form 21 warp strands using the Continuous Warp Method (see page 6).

2 Weave the design following the Bead Placement Chart (at left).

3 Hide the warp and weft threads using the method described on page 11.

4 Attach the findings using the method described on page 12.

Purple & Green Argyle Divided Necklace

By Carol C. Porter

1 Warp the loom with 25 threads using the Multiple Warp Method (see page 9).

2 Weave the design following the Bead Placement Chart (see below) and Dividing a Woven Piece (see page 12).

3 Join the ends of the necklace using the warp threads following the method described in Joining the Ends of the Necklace (see page 12).

4 Hide the weft threads using the method described on page 7.

5 Use the method described in Attaching Fringe to a Straight Edge (see page 13) to add a fringe to the bottom of the necklace, following the Bead Fringe Chart.

Techniques: Multiple Warp, Divided Necklace, Fringe
Beads: 24 across
Warp: 25

Supplies
- Beads (see Color Key and Bead Placement Chart)
- Nymo, size B in black
- Beading needle & threader
- Scissors

Color Key: Using 11/0 Toho Round Beads

 187 Celery Green

 249 Dark Green

 2108 Gilt Lined Iris

461 Royal

 557 Gold

Bead Fringe Chart
Repeat in reverse for left side of fringe

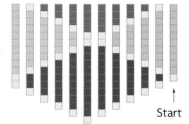

Start

Repeat until desired length is reached

Bead Placement Chart

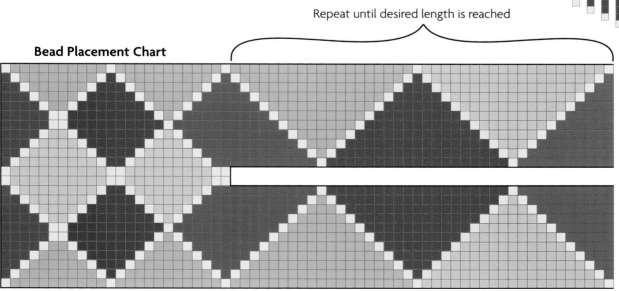

23

Blue & White Amulet Necklace

By Fran Ortmeyer

For bag:

1 Warp the loom with 37 threads using the Multiple Warp Method (see page 9).

2 Weave the design following the Bead Placement Chart (see below).

3 Hide the warp and weft threads using the method described on page 10.

4 Use the method described in Attaching Fringe to a Straight Edge (see page 13) to make a picot fringe following the Bead Fringe Chart.

5 Use the method described in Sewing Side Seams (see page 13) to sew the sides of the bag closed.

For strap:

1 Warp the loom with six 44" (112cm)-long threads using the Multiple Warp Method (see page 9).

2 Weave the design following the Bead Placement Chart (see below).

3 Hide the warp and weft threads using the method described on page 10.

4 Attach the strap to the bag using a method similar to sewing the flap for the "Bead-Tangle" Pendant Necklace (page 15). Pass a thread twice through the last row of beads on the strap and the first row of beads on the bag body. Repeat with the remaining end of the strap.

Techniques: Multiple Warp, Sewing Side Seams, Picot Fringe
Beads: 36 across (bag), 5 across (strap)
Warp: 37 (bag), 6 (strap)

Supplies
- Beads (see Color Key and Bead Placement Chart)
- Nymo, size B in white
- Beading needle & threader
- Scissors

Color Key: Using 11/0 Toho Round Beads

- 401 Opaque White
- 28 Dark Blue
- 163 Light Blue

Amulet Bag Strap

Repeat until desired length. End with 4 white rows.

Row 1 →

Bag Body

Bag body

Repeat 3 times

Fold

Flap

Row

Repeat pattern from start

Start ↓

Bead Fringe Chart

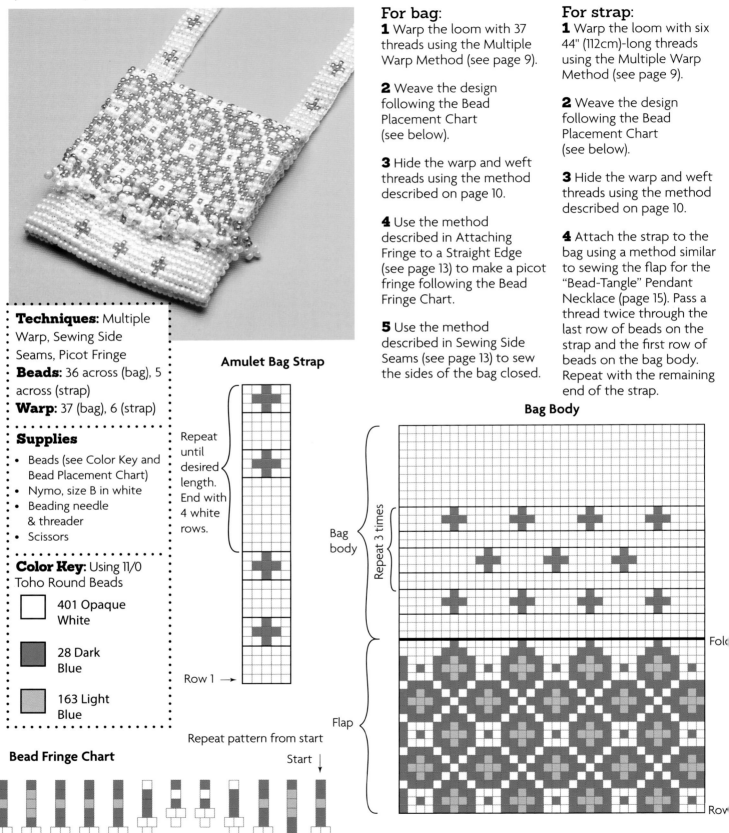

24

Bead Chart

Now that you have learned all the necessary techniques and completed the projects, you might be ready to begin creating your own jewelry designs. Toho beads come in a variety of finishes and colors. The charts on these pages are just a sampling of what's available. All the beads shown are Round, size 11/0. Use them to inspire your creativity. To see more bead colors and shapes, please visit www.tohobeads.net/sample/sample.html.

Col 1	Col 2	Col 3	Col 4	Col 5
1	22B	2114	50	120
2	22C	2115	51	121
2B	23	2116	52	122
2C	24	2117	53	123
3	25	2118	55	123D
3B	25B	2119	820	124
4	25C	2120		125
5	25D	2121	81	126
5B	26	2122	82	127
5C	26C	2123	83	128
5D	27	2124	84	129
6	27B	2125	85	132
6B	27BD	2126	86	133
7	28	2151S	87	
7B	29	2152S	88	141
7BD	30	2153S	89	142
8	31	2154S	90	143
9	32	2155S		144
9B	33	2156S	101	145L
10	34	2202	102	145
11	35	2203	103	146
12	36		103B	147
13	37	41	104	148
72	38	42	105	150
939	2100	42B	106	151
940	2101	42D	107	901
941	2102	43	108	902
942	2103	43D	108BD	903
1300	2104	44	109	904
2151	2105	45A	110	905
2152	2106	45	110B	906
2153	2107	46L	111	907
2154	2108	46	112	908
2155	2109	47	113	909
2156	2110	47D	114	910
	2111	48L	115	911
21	2112	48	116	917
22	2113	49	119	

25

● These colors may be changed by bleach or oxidation after a while.　★ These colors may wear off due to strong friction.
◆ These colors are nickel-plated.　▲ These colors may fade due to sunlight or UV rays.

Column 1

- 631
- 632
- 221 ●★
- 222 ●★
- 261
- 262
- 263
- 264
- 265
- 266
- 267 ▲
- 268
- 271
- 272
- 277 ▲
- 278 ▲
- 279 ▲
- 281
- 282
- 284
- 285 ▲
- 286 ▲
- 289
- 291
- 294
- 1014
- 1015
- 1812
- 1813
- 1814
- 1815
- 1816
- 321
- 322
- 323
- 324
- 325

Column 2

- 326
- 327
- 328
- 329
- 330
- 331
- 332
- 333
- 421
- 425
- 454
- 455
- 457
- 459
- 503
- 504
- 506
- 508
- 509
- ◆511 ●★
- ◆512 ●★
- ◆513 ●★
- ◆514 ●★
- ◆515 ●★
- ◆601 ●★
- ◆602 ●★
- ◆604 ●★
- ◆605 ●★
- ◆607 ●★
- ◆711 ●★
- ◆713 ●★
- ◆714 ●★
- ◆721 ●★
- 551 ●★
- 552 ●★
- 553 ★▲
- 554 ●★▲
- 556 ★▲

Column 3

- 557 ●★
- 558 ●★
- 559 ●★
- 560 ●★
- 561 ●★
- 562 ●★
- 563 ●▲
- 564 ★
- 565 ●★
- 701 ●
- ◆712 ●★
- ◆715 ●★
- 751 ●
- 752 ●
- 753 ●
- 754 ●
- 755 ●
- 756 ●
- 757 ●
- 758 ●
- ◆722 ●★
- 740 ●
- 741 ●
- 742 ●
- 743 ●
- 744 ●
- 745 ●
- 746 ●
- 747 ●
- 748 ●
- 749 ●
- 750 ●
- 1F
- 2CF
- 3CF
- 4F
- 5F

Column 4

- 5CF
- 6F
- 6CF
- 7BDF
- 8DF
- 9BF
- 11F
- 12F
- 13F
- 19F
- 72F
- 941F (423F)
- 940F
- 942F
- 21F ●
- 22F ●
- 26F ●
- 30F ●
- 31F ●
- 33F ●
- 2201 ●★
- 2204 ●★
- 41F
- 42BF
- 42DF
- 43F
- 43DF
- 44F
- 45F
- 46LF
- 46F
- 47F
- 47HF
- 48LF
- 48F
- 49F
- 51F
- 52F
- 53F

Column 5

- 55F
- 611
- 612
- 613
- 614
- 615
- 617
- 141F
- 142F
- 143F
- 144F
- 145F ▲
- 146F
- 148F
- 150F
- 151F
- 902F
- 910F
- 925F ▲
- 959F ▲
- 163BF
- 167BDF
- 177F
- 178F
- 761
- 768
- 191F ▲
- 967 ▲
- 968 ▲
- 969 ▲
- 970 ▲
- 972
- 973
- 974
- 975